clothes
around the world

Godfrey Hall

Wayland

Titles in this series:
Clothes Around the World
Festivals Around the World
Food Around the World
Houses Around the World
Musical Instruments Around the World
Shops and Markets Around the World
Toys and Games Around the World
Transport Around the World

Title page: Children in school uniform in Malaysia.

Series editor: Deb Elliott
Book design: Malcolm Walker
Cover design: Simon Balley

First published in 1995 by
Wayland (Publishers) Limited
61 Western Road, Hove
East Sussex BN3 1JD

© Copyright 1995 Wayland (Publishers) Limited

British Library Cataloguing in Publication Data
Hall, Godfrey
  Clothes. – (Around the World Series)
  I. Title II. Series
  391
ISBN 0 7502 1246 2

Typeset by Kudos Design Services
Printed and bound by Rotolito Lombarda s.p.a.

With thanks to Mike Theobald, Ennaimi Hazzim Abbas, King Fahad Academy, Dusseldorf Tourist Office, Joan and Harold Vidler.

Acknowledgements
The publishers would like to thank the following for allowing their pictures to be reproduced in this book:
APM 9; Damart 12; Eye Ubiquitous 4 (bottom, Tim Page), 6 (Philip Quirk),11 (Tim Page), 17 (Frank Leather), 22 (bottom, Greg Iland), 28 (bottom, Sean Aidan); Sally and Richard Greenhill 13; Robert Harding Picture Library 29 (bottom); Zul Mukhida 14 (top); Rex Features contents page (Patsy Fagan), top right cover and 5 (top, Eric Peltier) (bottom, A. Bradshaw), 7 (top, Maria Muinos), 10 (top, Philippe Millereau), 14 (bottom), 15 (top, Philip Goodliff), 20 (top), 22 (top), 23 (Nadai), 24 (both, Michael Friedel), 26, 29 (top, Brendan Beirn); Peter Sanders 10 (bottom); Tony Stone Worldwide bottom right cover, bottom left cover (Michael Scott), top left cover (Art Brewer), 4 (top, Tony Craddock), 8, 14, 18 (Michael Scott), 19, 20 (Doug Armand), 21 (Richard Passmore), 27 (top, Art Brewer), 28 (top); Alison Thomson 16 (bottom); Julia Waterlow 16 (top), 25, 27 (bottom).

the information store

📞 01603 773114
email: tis@ccn.ac.uk

---

21 DAY LOAN ITEM

Please return <u>on or before</u> the last date stamped above

CITY
COLLEGE
NORWICH

A fine will be charged for overdue items

Contents

Our clothes

The clothes people wear tell us a lot about who they are and where they live.

People who live in hot parts of the world wear clothes that keep them cool, like T-shirts and shorts made from cotton.

Hats offer shade from a hot, burning sun.

In cold parts of Canada, people wear clothes made from animal skins and fur.

Wearing lots of layers of clothes is another good way to keep warm in cold weather.

Hats

In hot countries, like Australia, people often wear hats with wide brims to protect them from the strong sunshine.

In the cold mountains of Peru, women wear thick, woollen hats which keep their heads warm.

Many boys who follow the Jewish religion wear a skullcap, called a *yarmulke,* from the age of three.

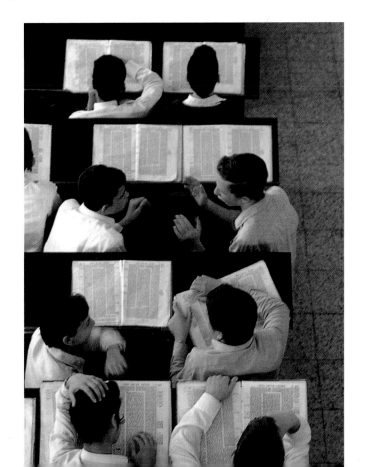

Shoes

In hot countries, such as India, women may wear sandals made from leather or rubber. Sandals let lots of cool, fresh air get to the feet.

Trainers are very popular with young people all over the world. These fashionable sports shoes are comfortable and look good.

Outdoor clothes

Children in Norway enjoy skiing in the snow. They wear padded anoraks and thick trousers, and gloves to keep their hands warm.

In hot countries, such as Saudi Arabia, people often wear white cotton clothes. These reflect the heat and keep them cool.

In Vietnam many people wear flowing cotton
shirts and loose trousers. These clothes let air
move around their bodies and are comfortable
in hot weather.

Underwear

In very cold parts of the world people often wear thermal underwear. This is made of a special material which traps heat around the body and keeps it warm.

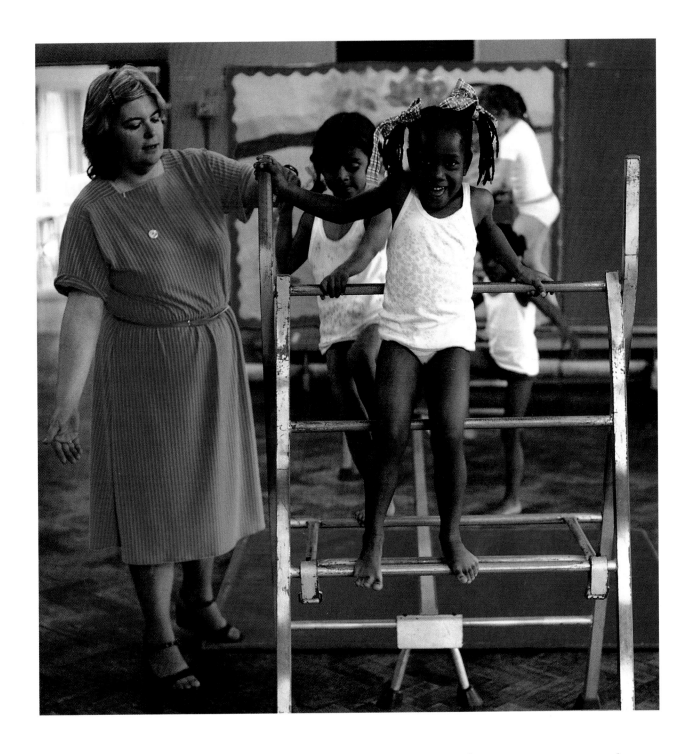

In Britain, children may have gym lessons wearing cotton vests and pants. This keeps them cool when doing lots of exercise.

Baby clothes

In many parts of the world, babies are dressed in all-in-one outfits with socks attached to them. These make the babies feel warm, snug and safe.

People sometimes wear special 'baby-carriers' attached to their backs or fronts. These help the baby to feel safe and snug against the mother or father's body.

In Guatemala, a mother may carry her baby in a brightly coloured shawl when she goes to the market.

Special occasions

People often dress up for festivals and religious occasions.

These Chinese men have dressed up in special costumes and have decorated their boat as part of the Dragon Boat festival.

In Indonesia, girls dress in black to celebrate weddings.

In Japan, the traditional kimono is worn by men and women at special events. It is a type of loose dress tied with a cord.

Traditional clothes

The weather can be very cold in Peru. Women and girls wear heavy woollen shawls called *aguayos*.

These Greek guards are wearing *fustanellas*, or kilts, which are their national costume.

Dressing up

During carnival time, children in Germany and The Netherlands dress up as clowns or wear funny hats.

Carnivals in the Caribbean and South America are very colourful and spectacular.

On the first Monday in May, English dancers known as Morris dancers wear white shirts and trousers decorated with ribbons and bells to celebrate the coming of summer.

Hot weather clothes

In hot weather, children love playing on the beach. They may wear just a swimsuit or shorts and a sunhat.

The sun in Australia can be very strong. People wear coloured sunscreen to protect their skin.

In Saudi Arabia women wear a flowing black cape called an *abaya*.

Cold weather clothes

When the weather is cold, we wear clothes that keep us snug and warm.

Lapland is an area of northern Europe. People who live there wear clothes made from reindeer skin to protect them from the ice-cold weather.

This boy lives in Quebec in Canada. His thick furry, hat keeps his ears and head warm and cosy.